Come to Work with Us in a
Hotel

by Jean and Ned Wilkinson

Foreword by Sam Levenson

Photography by Lee Fray
Reading Consultant: Sister Mary Julitta, O.S.F.,
Chairman, Reading Department,
Cardinal Stritch College, Milwaukee
Drawings by Roy Hurst
Design direction by Corchia, de Harak Inc., N.Y.

The authors and publisher gratefully acknowledge
the cooperation of Holiday Inns, Inc., Memphis,
Tennessee and the Holiday Inn, 644 N. Lakeshore
Drive, Chicago, IIIlnois 60611

Published by Sextant Systems, Inc.
Milwaukee, Wisconsin 53210

Library of Congress Catalog Card Number: 74-127858

© Copyright 1971, Sextant Systems, Inc., Milwaukee, Wisconsin

Distributed by Childrens Press, Inc., Chicago, Ill.

Sam Levenson

Dear Reader:

Work is one of the best words in the world. **Book,** too, is one of the best. A book about work is one of the best books in the world to have. You have that book in your hand now. Great!

Work can be fun, even when it is hard work. It is fun if it is what you want to do.

Every boy or girl wants to work some day. I know that you do. Most men and women work. Some work at home. Others work away from home. Some mothers stay home. They work for their family. This can be the hardest work of all. Just ask your mother.

To find the work you love you must plan ahead. You should plan to get along well with your job for a long time.

There are many kinds of jobs to pick from. You will have to work at picking the right work. You must use your head. That may be the hardest work of all. You cannot be lazy about work. That's how it works.

Each of us is good at something. There is nobody who is good for nothing. You can do things that **I** cannot do. You cannot always be what you would **like** to be. You can try to be what you **can** be. But whatever you can be you must do well. Good work makes you feel good. You earn your pay when you do a good job.

We want to help you find the work that will be right for you when you grow up. That's our job. Your job right now is to read this book. It pays. Your job right now is to learn about jobs.

In just a few pages you will begin to see pictures. They are pictures of young people working at grownup jobs. Try to see yourself in these jobs.

You will enjoy reading this book for many reasons:

- You have heard about these places and jobs.

- We tell you about the jobs in rhymes. You can read the little rhymes aloud. It's fun.

- The pictures were taken right where the real job takes place.

- You may look up the meaning of the new words in the back of the book.

- If you want to, you can act out the jobs. You can make little plays out of each job. You be the star. Some day you may be doing this work for real. That's even better than make believe jobs.

- You may want to try this game: Recite the rhyme and ask your friend to guess what your job is.

- Ask your parents to read along with you.

Your friend,

We are pretending we are grown.
Our jobs are grown-up too.
The pictures show you where we work,
The words tell what we do.

My name is Tom and I'm all thumbs
In everything I do.
I just can't get the job done right.
Does it look right to you?

Hotel

A hotel is the place
This book will show to you.
Just turn the page and come with us,
And we will take you through.

Doorman

I greet the guests at the front door
In weather cold or warm.
I open doors, call taxicabs.
I wear a uniform.

Room Clerk

I tell the guests which room is theirs,
Give them their mail and key.
My records tell their address, name,
How long their stay will be.

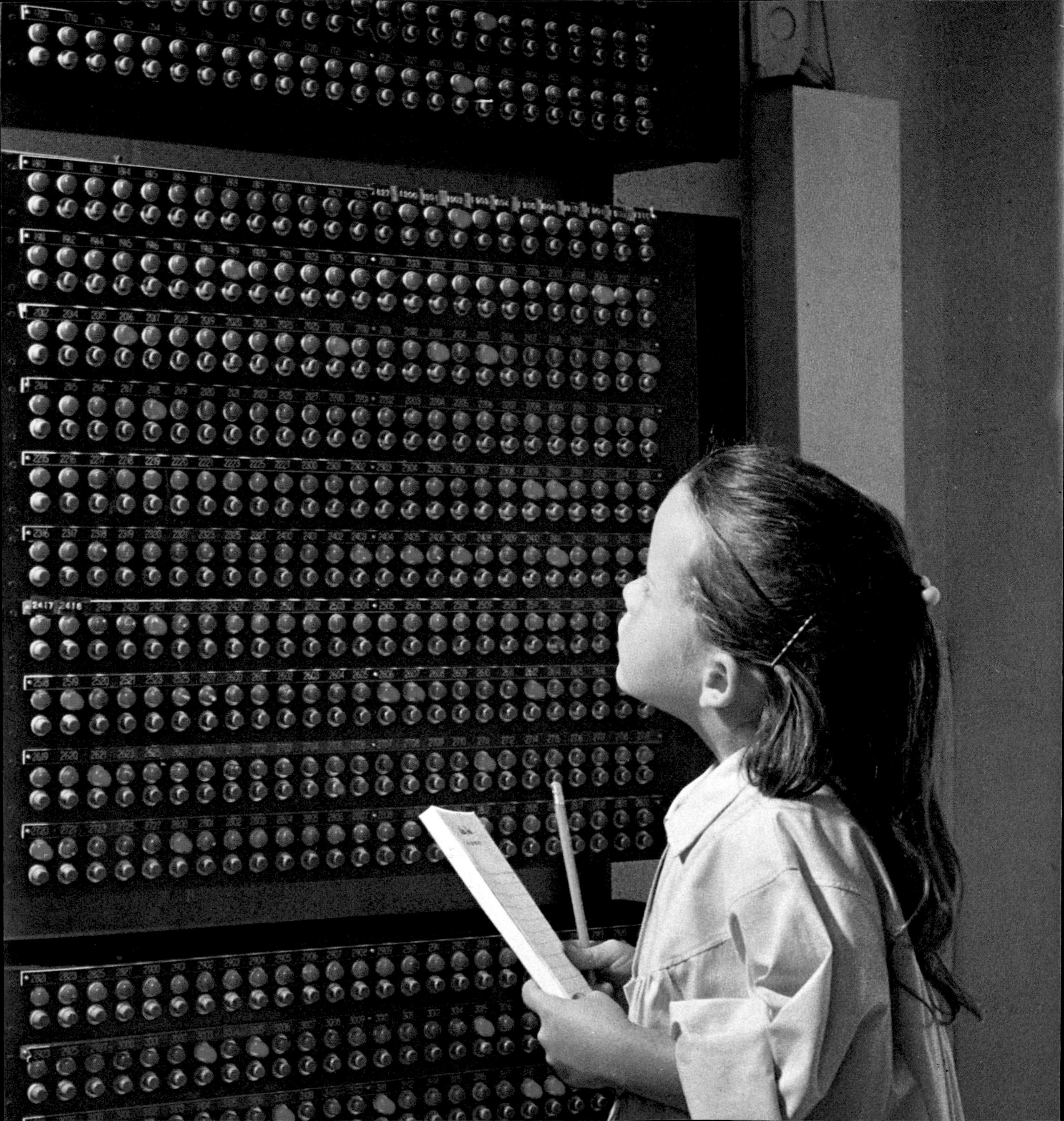

Housekeeper

I check the maids and what they do,
Assign work for each one.
My lights show me which rooms are clean
And which have to be done.

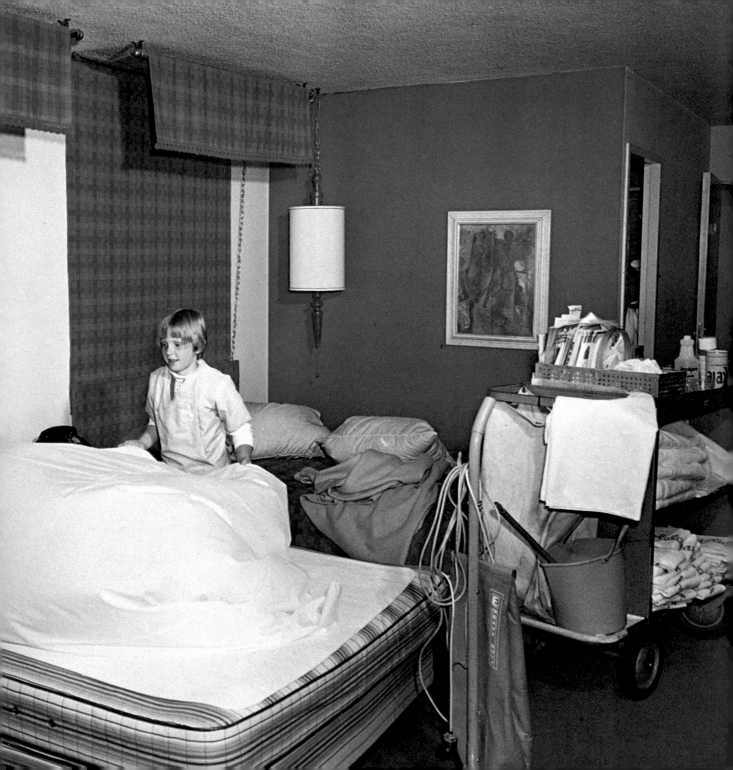

Maid

I make the beds and clean the rooms,
Each one in the same way.
I have a cart for my supplies.
I do this every day.

Commissary Manager

I buy and store the food and drinks
The restaurants will need,
I keep them fresh and clean, and know
How many we can feed.

19

Chef

Chef is the French word that means cook.
My helpers work with me.
I plan how food will taste and look,
And what the meals will be.

Head Waiter

I tell waiters and waitresses
Where their work will be done.
I find a table for the guests
And try to please each one.

Waitress - Waiter

I ask what people want to eat
And write down what they say.
I get it from the kitchen, then
I serve it from a tray.

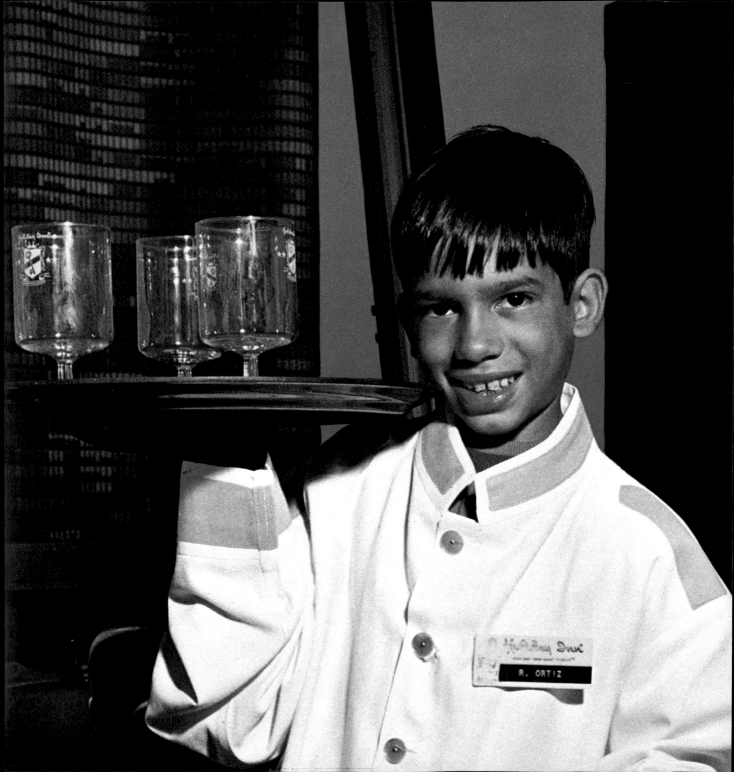

Bus Boy

I help waiters and waitresses
With things they have to do.
I set the tables for the guests,
Then clear them when they're through.

27

Dishwasher

I rub and scrub the pots and pans
To get them very clean.
Some dishes must be washed by hand
And others by machine.

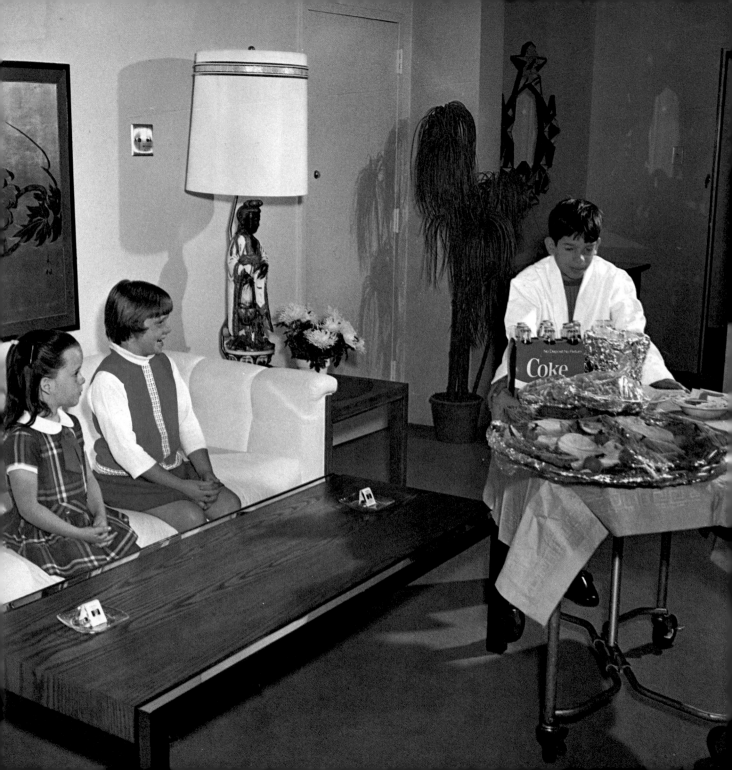

Room Service Waiter

I take to guests the food and drinks
They order on the phone.
I bring it to their room and then
Serve it to them alone.

Lifeguard

I watch the swimmers in the pool,
Make sure rules are obeyed.
For my job I have to know
Lifesaving and first aid.

Entertainer

I dance or sing, play music or
Tell funny jokes to you.
I give a show and you can come
And see me when I do.

Maintenance Man

I keep things working, looking good,
I paint, build or repair.
I have a shop where I can work.
The tools I need are there.

Catering Manager

I help plan meetings, parties, meals,
In big rooms that we rent.
I see that tables, chairs are there,
Order the food that's sent.

Cashier

I add up all the bills for guests.
They pay before they go.
I have a list to give to them.
It shows how much they owe.

Manager

I see that we do all we can
To rent our rooms each day.
I try to make our service please
The guests in every way.

GLOSSARY

address — place where one lives and where mail may be sent

assign — to give out work

cart — a wagon with wheels used to carry things

check — to make sure work is done right

clear — to take away

first aid — to give help right away to a person who is hurt

French — the language of the people of France

greet — to meet in a friendly way

guests — people who are staying at a hotel or eating in a restaurant

job — work

key — a piece of metal used to open a lock

lifesaving — a special way to help people who are in danger in the water

list — a piece of paper telling the things guests bought

machine — something with moving parts that does work

maids — woman worker who keeps rooms in order

means — what you want to say or show

meals — food to eat at one time

menu — a list of the food that is served at a meal

obey — to do what one is told

order — something that tells what to do

owe — to have to pay for something

phone — telephone

pool — a place with water used for swimming

pots — something used for cooking

paint — to cover with a kind of coloring

records — facts set down in writing

rent — to pay money for using something

repair — to put back in order

restaurant — a place where meals are served and sold to people

rule — tell what may and may not be done

scrub — wash by rubbing hard

serve — bring food or drink to someone

service — work people do for others

supplies — things on hand

taxicabs — cars with drivers who get paid for giving people rides

taste — the flavor of food or drink

through — done

tray — something flat used to carry or hold things

tools — anything used to do work

uniform — special clothes worn by workers

waiter/waitress — one who serves food or drinks

The authors and publisher gratefully acknowledge
the cooperation of Children's Press, Inc., in granting
permission to reprint selected definitions from the
"Dictionary of Basic Words," Copyright 1969, by
Regensteiner Publishing Enterprises, Inc.